Words

Corina Daniela Maereanu

BookLeaf
Publishing

Presentation by *BookLeaf Publishing*

Web: www.bookleafpub.com

E-mail: info@bookleafpub.com

ISBN: 9789395620925

First edition 2022

Preface

I don't believe in making wishes, in waiting on miracles, in saints or in sinners, in angels or devils. I don't believe in another life either. In my world, there's no souls and there's no designated destinies.

But I believe in how the trees shake their leaves, when the wind blows, guiding me. I believe in the sound of silence, and in hesitant smiles on the train, and in how two pairs of eyes can meet by chance, then look away, without a clue to why they crossed paths in the first place.

In my world, I'm inspired by the moon, by the truth, by mistakes, and by forgiveness. I'm inspired by how I believe there's no such thing as evil, just fear, and human nature that's been left to wither. And forever holding on to hope - to the hope that can heal even the most damaged of beings.

Family Portrait

I got arms like my mother,
To hold on to hope and carry on;
Legs like my father,
So I can wander away from home;

I run like my sister though,
Restless and fast,
One minute in the future
And another in the past,
Still present at times.

Only to stumble upon my own self,
Kind of like a rhythmless dance,
On an endless song
With all lyrics written in reverse.

Into the Unknown

I've been walking on a path
And I don't know where I'm going,
I turned left instead of right
On my way back home this morning.

For I've been walking all night
Following the stars and sunrise,
On an empty road, alone,
Far from everything I've ever known.

Yet when I was close to home,
I've decided that this time
I'll leave everything behind
And get lost in the unknown.

Ever since, I kept on going,
Guided by the river's flow,
And my mind is now at ease
Following the Northeast winds.

Dried Flower

Dried flower, you know you can never die,
You will bloom eternally in my mind...
Even after time is forever gone
I know you'll bloom again, somewhere,
somehow.

Gravity

Gravity, gravity,
Go leave your mark on me
So they can believe that
I lived beautifully.

Separate all that's right
From the soft spoken lies;
Stories overflowing
That I can leave behind;

Stories of a true past -
Joy, hardship, love or lust,
Everything in between,
I felt them all at once.

Gravity, gravity,
Go on and remind me,
What I feared most back then
Is what has set me free.

Missing Pieces

Warm grey tones that we used to shoot those pictures; warmth standing for love, and grey standing for realness.

We left pieces out of frame on purpose so that we'd be the only ones to remember. Some things are just not meant to be shared because the world would never understand the feeling.

And we couldn't care less if anyone would have chosen different. We'd still shoot the same pictures, capture the vision, get caught up in a moment elusively, and leave out the most beautiful pieces.

Nothing's as It Seems

Nothing's as it seems -
The blue birds faded in night skies again;
I would like to cry,
But it just won't rain enough until June.

Time cannot be stopped,
But moments can be frozen on paper.
Love can never die;
I started doubting if that's true lately…

Truth is no greater -
Life is nothing but heartbeats repeating;
They keep repeating,
Yet everything is still so different.

Soft

The path I chose is forward yet hollow,
Dark and thorough; only for a while though.
Like the river's tide when the flood recedes
Or flowers dew on a cold afternoon,
There's a light at the end of this path too.

The steps I take are soft, for the ground's ice.
If I look down now, I can see the cracks;
Beneath there's danger, and I'm a rolling dice.
If I look behind, might lose all power
To softly move past the darkest hours.

The breaths I take are soft, for the air's fire.
Birds whisper songs of a dragon's sorrow;
The moon will fade in about half an hour;
The water's dried out, my eyes are tired.
Will I hold my breath for another hour?

The words I speak are soft, unlike the path,
Never hollow, yet forward and thorough,
Sometimes dark, for it has to be followed
To find that light at the end of this path,
Even if I turn to fire and ice.

Even if I turn to fire and ice

I'll keep on moving forward down this path
That has guided this world's lost eyes and
minds,
Calmed down most violent rivers, winds, and
times;
And I'll move on softly, beyond its light.

Then I'll pick up roses and sunflowers,
Step on solid ground; dance for half an hour
In the rain, that floods the path I follow;
Leave my soft mind guided by each moon
phase;
Leave my soft body fade in pouring rains.

The Noodle Bar on the Other Side of Town

Seven dumplings on the go,
Still, most times I stay in,
Even when I wander away.

Noodles and her love for music
Kept swinging the hours by,
So I felt like home since then.

Few steamed buns on the stove,
Cold days bring warm memories, I'd say,
All steaming, sizzling, and day-dreaming.

A rice bowl on each table today!
How I've been waiting for this feeling!
Oh, how I could do this every evening!

In Spring

Just like butterflies in spring
We chase each other restlessly,
In an open field.

We hide and we seek
Where time and space can't reach;

And we don't know how to stop
Climbing trees, nor praising rivers;

And daisies don't know either
Whether it's us or the wind
That keeps giving them the shivers.

When You Look at Me

I see sharp, lone thorns and untamed life,
Both alike, allied, aligned…

Which so sharply caught your eye,
Together with the dark moon
Half brightened by the sun on a cloudless sky.

I see roses yet to bloom,
Not in sight but likely soon.
It's the calm before the storm;
Born, torn, turned into their form -

A simple, unremarkable light, yet outstandingly
truthful sight.

And I love how your world reveals itself to me.
I love to see, to feel, to be
All caught up in its every mystery…

Miss Me, Forget Me

Miss me, forget me

Miss me tomorrow, but please forget me today.
The sun will brighten the moon tonight
pridelessly,
Yet I will think about our memories proudly.
Still, when light falls on your eyes, just leave me
behind;
Don't look back for you shall loose yourself in
darkness;
When the light falls, don't stop and stare, just
look away;
Don't wait for me in the dazzling morning rain.
Stay safe; don't look up for the sky is now
cloudless…
Kiss me tomorrow, but please forgive me today.

And You Miss Me Too

August, July, June,
Still waiting for you;
Snows in the desert
And you miss me too.

Rainbow without rain,
Still waiting in vain;
Dried flower's in bloom
And you miss me too.

Ocean's in the sky
Waiting to say hi;
Cherries are now blue
And you miss me too.

Poet with no muse,
I sure do miss you…
Roses thorns are smooth
And you miss me too.

Calamari Sadness

Over fried calamari by the sea -
Kinda greasy,
But outrageously delicious…
Gotta let it be,
I ate it already.
Stomach might hurt but
I'll get over it.
Next time I'll eat
Spinach leaves sandwiches?

Yet I Choose to Feel Differently

Out of all of the stars in the night sky
That dare to shine,
I choose to watch the leaves of the tree
Growing right in front of me.

And though high and out of reach,
I most definitely feel everything;
And though I choose not to wish
On a shooting star,
I steadily and patiently
Watch the golden leaves fall.

And I most definitely see
How the golden leaves
Steadily and patiently start surrounding me;
Just as certain I am about
How this will happen every year.

Poppy Field Hues

Poppy seeds are dropping from winds of hope
back in depths and darkness, becoming life
again and growing happily ever after, in fields
not long forgotten by summer heat, yet suddenly,
there's no trace of breeze coming.

The lakes, blue-green, are splashing their
troubled water and shape the poppy field in
sunset red, simple white, and ocean blue hues
not matching the unimaginable, but never
crushing it's colour, shade, or matter, during
golden hour…

When just a another muse passes on its fragile
power to an artist writing their flaws, anger, joy,
and broadening narrow horizon, in poppy fields'
green, and red, and white, and blue colours.

Midnight Sun

Come be my midnight sun,
Warm me up when the heat is gone,
When I'm feeling numb,
Sing me an old song;
With the wind we'd be alone
And I'll think of you when the seasons change.

And I'll get lost in your untamed mind,
And that smile…
Could turn oceans into solid ground
Covered in blue flowers;
Could make my restless mind calm down for a
while,
Lost in the passing hours.

Hidden in Plain Sight

1:34 pm. Winter sun is out.
I drink hot tea and watch the people pass by.
They're rushing again, without destination;
I stand here, lost in the passing of time.

Then we are no different, after all…
Somehow we both dare to hide in plain sight;
While one shamelessly lights up the dark,
Another is running from dim light.

It's been this way since we can remember
But when to stop, and what for; we don't know.
Since time went by this way, we grew apart,
Seems I'm happier now that I'm alone.

In the nighttime, when darkness takes over,
Surrounded by strangers and my reflection,
In downtown's maze of half-litten windows
I can't help but notice fragments of affection.

The fine lines between past love and the present,
Or between my fingers and my cold arms
Reveal fragile truths hidden in plain sight,
That time has gifted to me as my charms.

Where Have You Been?

Where have you been?
The moon seemed to be falling;
There is a spark
In blues of broken loving.

I heard flowers
Calling out my name each day,
I was never home,
I was not sure what to say;

Nighttime was dark,
Darker than the alleys,
Where I lost all
Hidden in the depths of valleys;

I could see clouds
Gathering above the old trees;
Would I still pretend
That I did not know how it feels?

The rivers sang
Songs of a love in the rain;
I was just standing
Waiting by a passing train;

The blue birds danced,
The blue skies lifted their sorrow,
Fallen on the ground
In drops that counted an hour.

I've been away…
Have you seen me anywhere?
I could not find
Myself, in haze and cold air.

Leaves changed colours,
Thin moon dust must have fallen;
Thieves have rearranged
The thoughts that they've stolen.

Today at dawn
The light crossed in seven shades;
I'll stay right here
Until the 'coming darkness fades;

Dragonflies paint
Now legends of rivers and time.
Where have I been?
I could not once leave my mind...

White Pages

I want to write about forget-me-nots
On white pages;
I want to paint twenty-seven blue dots
Until each season changes.

When the wind blows making flowers shiver,
Past this blue field,
I want to write of ripples on the river,
And eat the oranges you peeled.

Today, again, I want to stay up all night,
Noticing stages,
I will write about the sky turning bright
On these faded white pages.

Patient

Patient
But a little restless;
Help me
Notice
How our stubborn love unfolds;
Break my
Defences
I don't know how warmth feels anymore.

Sing your favourite song to me
And I'll be
Listening on the go
When I run away
From you,
My love…
I'll come back,
I'll come back to hold you,
I'll come back to sing with you.

9 789395 620925